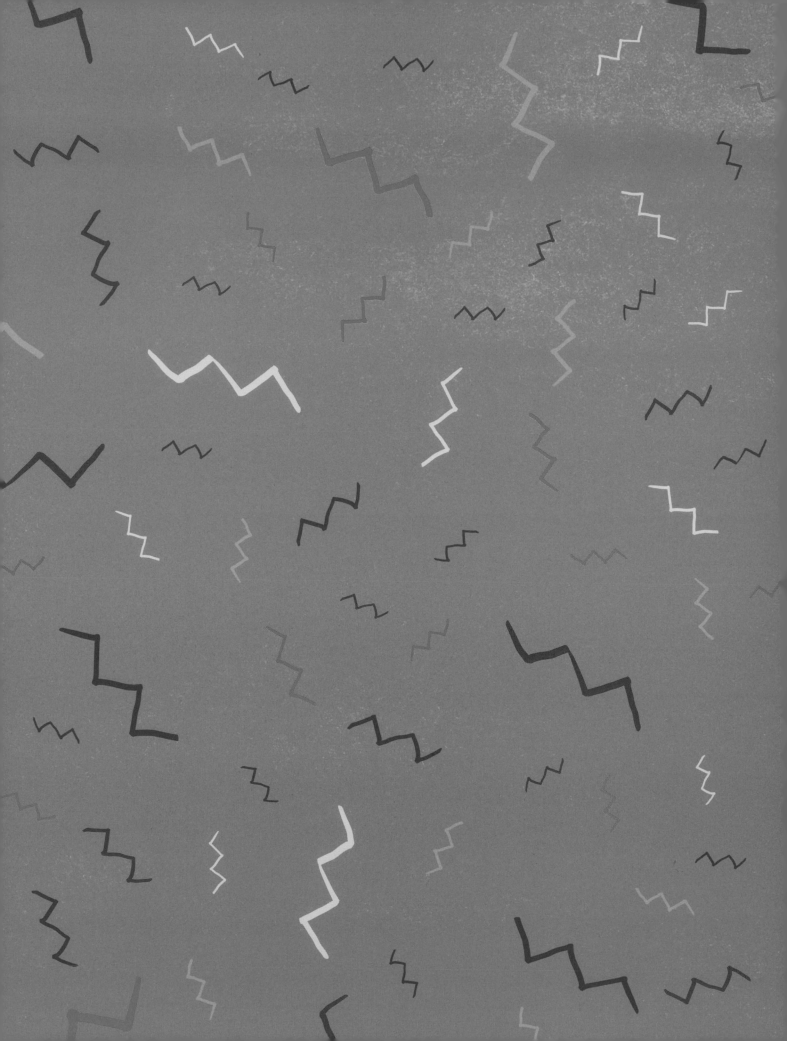

BLACK ARTISTS SHAPING THE WORLD

SHARNA JACKSON   ILLUSTRATED BY MARILYN ESTHER CHI

14 STORIES OF CREATIVITY

t&h

JOANA CHOUMALI 14-15

LUBAINA HIMID 10-13

LARRY ACHIAMPONG 16-19

ROSEMARY KARUGA 20-21

NICK CAVE 22-25

ZIZIPHO POSWA 8-9

BLACK ARTISTS SHAPING THE WORLD IS A CELEBRATION!

CHRIS OFILI 4-7

It's a party to praise some of the many talented Black artists creating exciting and important work today. This book is your invitation to join us. Come in! Meet the artists and discover how their art shows how they think and feel.

These artists are brilliant at making us look at and think about art and life. They work in many different ways and explore all kinds of ideas. Their talents shape our world, too.

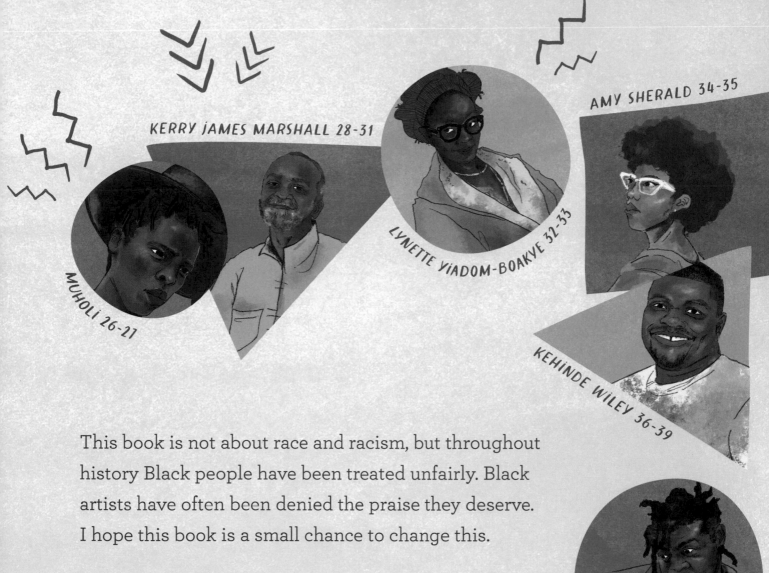

MUHOLI 26-27

KERRY JAMES MARSHALL 28-31

LYNETTE YIADOM-BOAKYE 32-33

AMY SHERALD 34-35

KEHINDE WILEY 36-39

This book is not about race and racism, but throughout history Black people have been treated unfairly. Black artists have often been denied the praise they deserve. I hope this book is a small chance to change this.

It was very difficult to choose just 14 artists. Dr. Zoé Whitley and I thought about the many ways of creating —photography, painting, ceramics, installations, textiles, and everything in between—and chose some of the very best artists working with these types of art.

I hope *Black Artists Shaping the World* does two things. One—inspire you to find out more about these artists. Two—encourage you to create in any way you want, no matter where or who you are.

SHARNA JACKSON

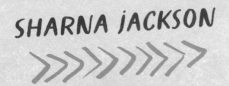

YINKA SHONIBARE 40-41

FAITH RINGGOLD 42-45

CHRIS
OFILI

Painting for justice

In 1998, artist Chris Ofili created a tribute to Stephen Lawrence, a young man who had been murdered in a racist attack in London five years before. Stephen was simply waiting for a bus.

No Woman, No Cry is the title of Chris's tribute, and it is inspired by Stephen's mother, Doreen. For years, Doreen fought for justice—not just for her son, but also for other victims of racist crimes. Watching interviews of Doreen, Chris saw her personal sorrow, and also the sadness many people feel when they lose their loved ones.

No Woman, No Cry has the same name as an iconic song by reggae musician Bob Marley. In that song, Marley tells a woman not to be sad. In Chris's work, the woman weeps. There are photographs of Stephen in each of her tears.

Chris uses lots of layers and materials in his work, including resin, glitter, and different types of paint. He has famously used elephant dung in some of his creations, including this one. He liked the idea of placing earthy materials next to beautiful art. Here, he dried and varnished the dung and placed it on the woman's necklace like a locket. Lumps of it are also used to support the painting when it is placed against a wall. Chris stuck map pins into these lumps to spell out the title of the work.

He also used a special luminous paint, which you can only really see in the dark. At night, you can read the words "R.I.P. Stephen Lawrence 1974-1993" written across the canvas.

No Woman, No Cry, 1998

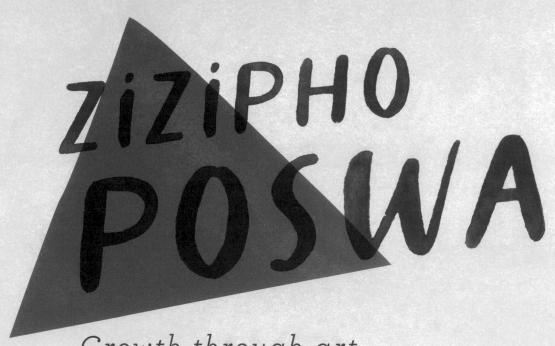

ZIZIPHO POSWA

Growth through art

Zizipho Poswa is a South African ceramic sculptor, but she didn't always work with clay. She started as a textile designer, hand-painting colorful patterns onto fabrics.

This pair of sculptures, *Ukukhula I* (radiant red, with small scraps of clay from Zizipho's studio) and *Ukukhula II* (bright blue, with flashes of red and spiky triangles), are kind of like siblings—from the same family, but different. For Zizipho, they also play with ideas that can seem like opposites, such as feminine and masculine, protection and aggression, and old and new.

Ukukhula is an isiXhosa word that means "growth." These sculptures are big—both over three feet tall—but the title is not just about their size. They also tell the story of Zizipho's journey of growth in the art world.

Ukukhula II, 2018

Ukukhula I, 2018

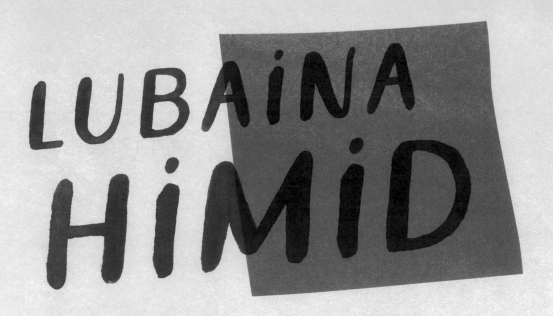

LUBAINA HiMiD

Giving a voice to the past

Lubaina Himid was born in Zanzibar and moved
to England as a baby. When she visited museums
in Europe, she noticed something about
the grand paintings of old, rich
families. She saw that Black
people—if they were there
at all—were almost always
enslaved workers or
servants. They would
be at the edge, holding
trays or teapots, but
never at the center.

My name is Effiong
They call me John
I used to make rings for royal fingers
Now I make shoes for ladies' feet
But I have the gold

Lubaina wanted to take these
people out of the paintings and
give them names, bodies, and lives.
She wanted them to share their stories.

In her installation, *Naming the Money*, from
2004, Lubaina created 100 life-size painted
cut-outs of people. On their back, in a short poem,
each person tells you their real name, then the
name given to them by their masters. They
tell you what they used to do, and what they're
forced into doing now. Then, they tell you something
that shows they are being positive, and making the
most of their terrible situation.

In a gallery, a soundtrack with music from all over the world plays
around the figures. Lubaina reads out the poems—her people have
finally been given a voice.

Naming the Money, 2004

JOANA CHOUMALI

Dreams at the first light of dawn

Every morning between five and seven, Joana Choumali walks around Abidjan in Côte d'Ivoire, a country in West Africa. While her family sleeps, she captures the landscapes and buildings of the city with her camera, and snaps the people she sees on the streets with her smartphone. This is a magical time for Joana.

The work, *Because We Actually Played Outside As Kids,* is part of a series called *Alba'hian*. This word means "the first light of the day" in the Agni language. It describes the feelings that arrive with the start of a new day, which Joana wants to capture in her work.

When the sun has fully risen, Joana returns to her studio to start creating her images. She prints her photographs onto canvas, then adds layers of

Because We Actually Played Outside As Kids, 2020

see-through fabric to recreate the light of dawn and dreamy morning fog. She adds gold paints, then begins to sew in brightly colored threads, weaving her feelings into her work.

Her photographs are taken quickly, but Joana sews slowly. Each piece can take months to make. She is patient, but she doesn't plan. Joana lets her photographs guide her, and her imagination run free!

LARRY ACHIAMPONG

Make the future you want to see

"Sankofa" is something Larry Achiampong's mother used to say when he was growing up in East London. This Ghanaian Twi word roughly means "go back and get it." Larry loved the thought of time travel, and developed "Sanko-time"—an idea that someone can use the past to prepare for the future.

Pan African Flag for
The Relic Travellers'
Alliance, 2017

This was the start of *Relic Traveller*—a project set in a fictional world that began in 2017, and still carries on today.

In Larry's futuristic world, fifty-four African countries have joined together as a group, called the Pan-African Union. Their goal is to make sure the future is fair, and learn from the mistakes of the past. To do this, the Union sends explorers with space-travel tech across the world to collect clues. The travelers seek out the stories of people from Africa who were treated terribly. These stories help the Union to understand what happened, and to heal.

Relic Traveller is not just a story. It exists as short films, music, performances, and even specially made flags. Each flag has fifty-four stars, one for each African country. Larry always uses four colors: black for the people in the Union, red to represent their blood, green to reflect the land and environment, and yellow as a promise of a bright future. The flags have been flown in public spaces internationally. This is very important to him because he does not want his work to just be shown inside galleries. He wants as many people as possible to see it and feel connected to it.

Still from *Relic 2*, 2017

Woman Standing, 1997

ROSEMARY KARUGA

A lifetime of achievements

Rosemary Karuga is known as the "mother of East African art."
She was born in Kenya in 1928 and became the first woman ever
to go to the School of Fine Art at Makerere University in Uganda,
in 1950. She studied design, painting, and sculpture, but didn't have
much success selling her work. So, when she graduated, Rosemary
returned to Kenya to be an art teacher.

Rosemary only started sharing her work when she retired in 1987.
Her bright collages told stories from her life, and were made
from whatever was around her house. She cut out colored
shapes from newspapers, magazines, and packaging.

At sixty years old, Rosemary achieved her dream of
becoming a full-time artist. After she illustrated
a book in 1990, her work became popular
and well-known across the world.

Rosemary sadly died in February
2021 but she remains an
inspiration to many.

NICK CAVE

Play, perform, protect

A terrible event happened in 1991. A young Black man named Rodney King was violently attacked by members of the Los Angeles Police Department. This led to riots in the city in 1992. Since that year, the African American artist Nick Cave has created over five hundred "Soundsuits"— a colorful series of sculptures you can wear. Rodney's attack had a big effect on Nick, and on his work.

Nick thought about how scary it can be to be Black in the world when some people want to hurt you just because of the color of your skin. He decided to create a suit of armor out of twigs and wire for protection. The twigs made noises as he moved, and the first "Soundsuit" was born. Since then, every suit has been made by hand from a range of materials including fake fur and feathers, buttons and beads, dolls, and doilies.

Soundsuits are interesting because they make people look, but they hide whoever's inside. On the inside they are safe and private, but from the outside they are larger than life and take up lots of space.

Soundsuits are not just playful costumes, though. They celebrate African and African American traditions, Mardi Gras parades, and rituals. People can wear them to dance and perform. Wearing a Soundsuit can make you feel free! Free from being judged, and free from judging others.

Soundsuit #2, 2009

MUHOLI

Your identity matters

Zanele Muholi uses the word "they", instead of "she" or "he". They also like to be called by their last name. Muholi uses photography to remind themselves—and others who have been treated unfairly in the past—that they exist and that they matter.

Muholi's work is often about their life. This self-portrait, *Bester I, Mayotte*, is a great example. "Bester" was Muholi's mother's first name. "Mayotte" is the place where Muholi took this photograph in 2015.

Muholi was the youngest of eight children. When Muholi's father died just after they were born, Bester had to work very hard, spending long hours away from her family. She worked for a white family under apartheid—a terrible system that meant people in South Africa were divided by the color of their skin and forced to live apart. Bester worked like this for forty-two years.

Bester I, Mayotte, 2015

In the photograph, Muholi stares at us. Their black skin is rich and deep. If you look quickly, you might think they are wearing bold accessories and clothing. But look again—Muholi's earrings and crown are clothespins, and a doormat is around their shoulders. These are not just household objects, and Muholi is not just trying to be fashionable. The objects are used to tell us about Black African women's experiences throughout history. The work is a tribute to Muholi's mother, and to domestic workers across the world.

KERRY JAMES MARSHALL

Black is beautiful

The African American artist Kerry James Marshall is one of the world's greatest living painters. He's famous for using a deep black color to paint his people. Kerry wants to make sure that Black people are seen in paintings and included in art history.

Kerry paints everyday places like living rooms, restaurants and barber shops. In *School of Beauty, School of Culture*, created in 2012, he opens the door to a beauty school. For many Black people, beauty salons are like community centers—the conversations around you are just as exciting as your haircut! There, you don't just learn about the business of beauty, you also talk about traditions and tell tales. They are fun, safe spaces.

Kerry's painting is a celebration of Black beauty. "Black is Beautiful" was a movement started in the 1960s against the racist idea that Black people are ugly. In Kerry's painting, posters on the walls exclaim "dark" and "lovely"—which is also the name of a Black haircare company. Kerry's figures are just that—dark and lovely.

But there is a strange part of the painting that only the children seem to see. They are pointing at a crooked image of the blond-haired, blue-eyed Princess Aurora from Disney's Sleeping Beauty. Kerry is saying that ideas of white beauty are everywhere, even when Black beauty surrounds them.

School of Beauty, School of Culture, 2012

LYNETTE YIADOM-BOAKYE

Use your imagination

Lynette Yiadom-Boakye is a British painter who works in a very interesting way. Look at *A Concentration,* which she painted in 2018. You probably think she visited a ballet studio and studied the dancers, right? She didn't! They're not real people. Her characters are fictional, and she calls them "figments." There are always people in Lynette's work, but they are definitely not portraits. She works from her imagination and from images she has found to create characters.

When she begins a new piece, Lynette knows roughly what she wants to see, and then lets her paints guide her work. She also works very quickly! She used to produce a painting in a single day—not only because she says she's impatient, but also because she finds it harder to come back to her work when the paint is dry.

A Concentration, 2018

Most of the people in Lynette's paintings are similar. They wear simple clothes and are set against simple backgrounds. They don't tend to wear shoes because shoes make you think of a specific time or place. Also, Lynette's figments are Black but this is not a protest or a celebration. As a Black person herself, Lynette's Blackness is not something different or special; it just is what it is.

AMY SHERALD

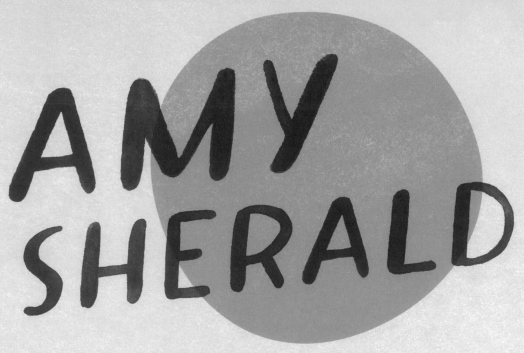

Inspire and be inspired

In 2018, Amy Sherald became the very first African American woman to create a presidential portrait—a tradition started in 1797. The woman in her painting, Michelle Obama, is a lawyer and a writer. Her husband was the 44th president of the United States, so she became the first African American First Lady. Because of these "firsts," it's a very important painting. Michelle chose Amy to paint the portrait herself, saying she was "blown away by the boldness of her colors."

By using gray, Amy takes away people's thoughts and feelings about Black skin and lets us just see the person. Old black-and-white photographs of her grandmother inspired Amy to use gray.

First Lady Michelle Obama, 2018

In this portrait, the shape of Michelle's dress makes her look like a mighty mountain. Some people think the colors and shapes on the dress look like the brilliant and bold quilts made by descendants of enslaved Africans in Gee's Band, Alabama.

Amy's painting was hung in the Smithsonian in Washington, but quickly had to be moved to a bigger room because so many visitors came to see it! Amy wants to inspire people with her portraits and her painting did just that.

KEHINDE WILEY

Take a closer look

Kehinde Wiley would visit museums and galleries on weekends in Los Angeles when he was growing up. He was fascinated by the large portraits of rich white people—their powdered wigs, pearls, and the puppies sitting proudly on their laps. He was struck by the way these paintings showed how powerful the people were. He began thinking about how Black people could appear in art like this and how they could be seen as "heroes."

Napoleon Leading the Army over the Alps, created by Kehinde in 2005, is an equestrian portrait—a painting of a person on a horse. It is based on *Napoleon Crossing the Alps at the Great Saint Bernard Pass*, painted in around 1800 by the French painter Jacques-Louis David. Both titles relate to the French leader Napoleon Bonaparte and both mention the Alps mountains but there are big differences.

The men in both paintings are riding the same horse and pointing upward with their right hand—but Kehinde's portrait features a young Black man. Where David's Napoleon wears a general's uniform, a hat, long leather boots, and a gauntlet, Kehinde's Napoleon wears camouflage, a bandana, Timberland boots, and a wristband. The backgrounds are also different: in David's painting the French army is climbing a mountain, but in Kehinde's painting the background is a red and gold tapestry.

Jacques-Louis David wrote the last name of his sitter, "BONAPARTE" on a rock in his painting, along with the names of other military commanders. Kehinde Wiley, in his version, adds the last name of his own model, "WILLIAMS."

Jacques-Louis David, *Napoleon Crossing the Alps at the St Bernard Pass*, late 18th–early 19th century

Kehinde Wiley, *Napoleon Leading the Army Over the Alps*, 2005

YINKA SHONIBARE

Spread your wings

When Yinka Shonibare was a student, and a teacher asked him why he didn't make "real" African art, he wondered what they meant. Yinka is both European and African. He grew up in England and Nigeria, and can speak Yoruba and English. He is interested in the relationship between the two continents, and you can see that in his work.

Butterfly Kid (Girl) IV, made in 2017, is a sculpture of a child. Her head is a black globe, with a map of the night sky on it—but the stars are named after butterflies. She has bright wings on her back and wears colorful shoes, tights, and a bold dress made from Ankara fabric.

People often think Ankara fabric is African, but it's more complicated than that. It was first made in 19th century Europe, but its designs were based on patterns from Indonesia. It was then sold in West Africa. Today, these fabrics are made in England and the Netherlands. See? Not simply African!

Butterfly Kid (Girl) IV, 2017

But in this work, Yinka also looks beyond our world, and into the future. This sculpture was inspired by climate change—and how we might escape it. If we can no longer live on Earth, then perhaps, like the Butterfly Kids, we may be able to grow wings and fly away.

FAITH RINGGOLD

Fly high and tell your own story

When Faith Ringgold was a little girl in the 1930s, she would visit Tar Beach—that's what she called the roof of her family's New York apartment. On summer nights, Faith and her brother and sister would lie on blankets, eat snacks, and stare at the stars. Her parents would sit, talk, and play cards. Faith would stare at the George Washington Bridge, wishing she could fly over it.

Faith has always loved art. She started by painting flowers and plants but, in the 1950s and '60s, the world began to change. Black people, who have been treated unfairly throughout history, protested for equal rights. Faith joined in the fight, and painted pictures about the injustices she saw. She then created other art—sculptures, and masks that she would wear on stage. Faith also traveled to Europe and Africa, and became a teacher. She was very busy!

All of these different things led Faith to making quilts. She added words to them to tell stories. These story quilts are what she is most famous for now—but she's been interested in making quilts for a long time. Faith would watch her mother sew when she was small, back in the days when she would go to Tar Beach.

Faith created this quilt, *Tar Beach*, in 1988. In her story, we follow the fantastic dreams of Cassie Louise Lightfoot, who, on a summer night at Tar Beach, flies over a bridge. Cassie proudly says, "I am free to go where I want to for the rest of my life."

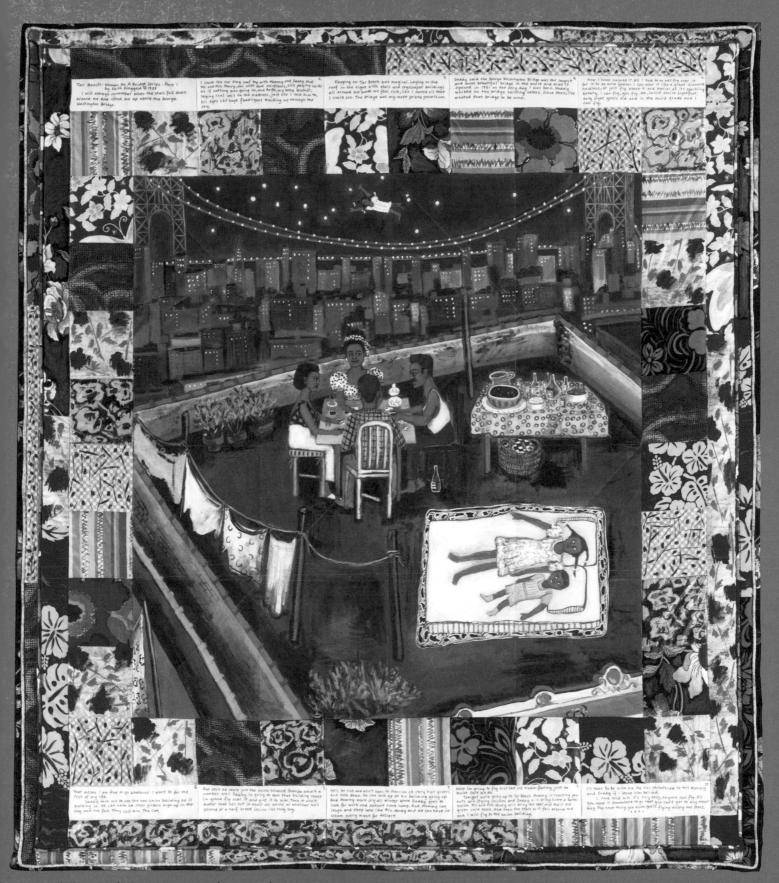

Tar Beach (Part I of Woman on a Bridge series), 1988

GLOSSARY

apartheid—a system created by white rulers to separate white people from non-white people ("apartheid" is an Afrikaans word, meaning "apartness"); based on white supremacy (the idea that white people are superior to and should dominate non-white people), it lasted in South Africa from 1948 to 1994; segregation in the U.S. was a similar idea, also discriminating against non-white people

canvas—a surface for painting on; usually a specially prepared piece of cloth that has been stretched tightly over a frame

ceramicist—an artist who works with clay

collage—the technique of using different individual elements to create a single image or artwork; the finished work is also called a collage

equestrian portrait—a picture of a person on a horse; an equestrian statue would be a sculpture of a person on a horse

installation—a three-dimensional work of art, often large and designed for a specific space

life-size—an artwork that is the actual size of a person or object in real life

movement (art)—a group of artists who share interests and ideas that influence the type of art they make

Pan-African—a term that unites all African countries or peoples together

performance—an artwork that consists of pre-planned or spontaneous actions, carried out by the artist or by participants

portrait—a picture or sculpture of a person, who is usually real rather than imaginary

race—a categorization of humans, usually based on shared physical characteristics such as skin color

racism—discrimination against a person or people of a certain categorization, often based on their skin color

resin—a material that can either be natural (derived from plants or insects) or synthetic (manufactured industrially); it is sometimes used to make artworks such as sculptures

sculpture—a three-dimensional work of art, often—but not always—carved in a material such as marble, bronze, or wood

self-portrait—a portrait that an artist makes of themselves

series—several artworks that belong in the same grouping, often sharing the same subject matter

sitter—a person who poses for a portrait

soundtrack—a recording of music or sound

studio—the place where an artist works

title—the name an artist gives to an artwork they have made

LIST OF ARTWORKS

Page 6: **Chris Ofili**, *No Woman, No Cry*, 1998.
Oil paint, acrylic paint, graphite, polyester resin, printed paper, glitter, map pins, and elephant dung on canvas, 243.8 × 182.8 × 5.1 cm (96 × 72 × 2 ⅛ in.). Tate. © Chris Ofili, courtesy Victoria Miro, London

Page 7: **Chris Ofili**, *No Woman, No Cry*, night-time view with 'R.I.P. Stephen Lawrence 1974–1993' visible.
Tate. © Chris Ofili, courtesy Victoria Miro, London

Page 9: **Zizipho Poswa**, *Ukukhula I* (right) and *Ukukhula II* (left), 2018. Glazed stoneware, 33 × 33 × 102 cm (13 × 13 × 40¼ in.) and 46 × 46 × 106 cm (18 ⅛ × 18 ⅛ × 41¾ in.), respectively. Collection of the Los Angeles County Museum of Art. Gift of the 2019 Decorative Arts and Design Acquisitions Committee (DA2), with additional support from Debbie and Mark Attanasio and Allison and Larry Berg. Photo Hayden Phipps, courtesy Southern Guild

Page 11: **Lubaina Himid**, *Figure from Naming the Money*, 2004.
Courtesy the artist and Hollybush Gardens, London. Photo Andy Keate

Page 12-13: **Lubaina Himid**, *Naming the Money*, 2004.
Plywood, acrylic, mixed media, dimensions variable. Installation view of "Navigation Charts," Spike Island, Bristol, 2017. Courtesy the artist, Hollybush Gardens, London, and National Museums, Liverpool. Photo Stuart Whipps

Page 15: **Joana Choumali**, *Because We Actually Played Outside as Kids*, from the series Alba'hian, 2020.
Mixed media, 80 × 80 cm (31½ × 31½ in.). © Joana Choumali

Page 16: **Larry Achiampong**, *Pan African Flag for The Relic Travellers' Alliance*, 2017.
Installation. © Larry Achiampong. All rights reserved, DACS/Artimage 2021. Courtesy the artist

Page 17-18: **Larry Achiampong**, *Relic 2*, 2017.
4K color video still. © Larry Achiampong. All rights reserved, DACS/Artimage 2021. Supported by Arts Council England. Courtesy the artist and Copperfield London

Page 20: **Rosemary Karuga**, *Woman Standing*, c. 1997.
Collage on paper, 40 × 30 cm (15¾ × 11⅞ in.). Red Hill Art Gallery, Nairobi. Courtesy the artist's estate

Page 25: **Nick Cave**, *Soundsuit*, 2009.
Synthetic hair, 146.4 × 66 × 50.8 cm (97 × 26 × 20 in.). © Nick Cave. Courtesy the artist and Jack Shainman Gallery, New York

Page 27: **Zanele Muholi**, *Bester I, Mayotte (Hail the Dark Lioness)*, 2015 from the series "Somnyama Ngonyama, Hail the Dark Lioness," 2012–ongoing.
Gelatin silver print, 100 × 72 cm (30 × 28 in.). Stedelijkmuseum, Amsterdam. © Zanele Muholi. Courtesy Stevenson, Cape Town/Johannesburg, and Yancey Richardson, New York

Page 30-31: **Kerry James Marshall**, *School of Beauty, School of Culture*, 2012.
Acrylic and glitter on unstretched canvas, 274.3 × 401.3 cm (108 × 158 in.). Birmingham Museum of Art, Birmingham, AL. Museum purchase with funds provided by Elizabeth (Bibby) Smith, the Collectors Circle for Contemporary Art, Jane Comer, the Sankofa Society, and general acquisition funds (2012.57). © Kerry James Marshall. Courtesy the artist and Jack Shainman Gallery, New York

Page 33: **Lynette Yiadom-Boakye**, *A Concentration*, 2018.
Oil on linen, 200.3 × 250.2 cm (78⅞ × 98½ in.). © Lynette Yiadom-Boakye. Courtesy the artist, Jack Shainman Gallery, New York, and Corvi-Mora, London

Page 35: **Amy Sherald**, *First Lady Michelle Obama*, 2018.
Oil on linen, 183.2 × 152.7 cm (72⅛ × 60⅛ in.). National Portrait Gallery, Smithsonian Institution; gift of Kate Capshaw and Steven Spielberg; Judith Kern and Kent Whealy; Tommie L. Pegues and Donald A. Capoccia; Clarence, DeLoise, and Brenda Gaines; Jonathan and Nancy Lee Kemper; The Stoneridge Fund of Amy and Marc Meadows; Robert E. Meyerhoff and Rheda Becker; Catherine and Michael Podell; Mark and Cindy Aron; Lyndon J. Barrois and Janine Sherman Barrois; The Honorable John and Louise Bryson; Paul and Rose Carter; Bob and Jane Clark; Lisa R. Davis; Shirley Ross Davis and Family; Alan and Lois Fern; Conrad and Constance Hipkins; Sharon and John Hoffman; Audrey M. Irmas; John Legend and Chrissy Teigen; Eileen Harris Norton; Helen Hilton Raiser; Philip and Elizabeth Ryan; Roselyne Chroman Swig; Josef Vascovitz and Lisa Goodman; Eileen Baird; Dennis and Joyce Black Family Charitable Foundation; Shelley Brazier; Aryn Drake-Lee; Andy and Teri Goodman; Randi Charno Levine and Jeffrey E. Levine; Fred M. Levin and Nancy Livingston, The Shenson Foundation; Monique Meloche Gallery, Chicago; Arthur Lewis and Hau Nguyen; Sara and John Schram; Alyssa Taubman and Robert Rothman. © National Portrait Gallery, Smithsonian Institution

Page 38: **Jacques-Louis David**, *Napoleon Crossing the Alps at the Great Saint Bernard Pass*, late 18th–early 19th century.
Oil on canvas, 259 × 221 cm (102 × 87⅛ in.). Châteaux de Malmaison et Bois-Préau, Rueil-Malmaison, France. Photo RMN-Grand Palais (musée des châteaux de Malmaison et de Bois-Préau)/Franck Raux

Page 39: **Kehinde Wiley**, *Napoleon Leading the Army Over the Alps*, 2005.
Oil on canvas, 274.3 × 274.3 cm (108 × 108 in.). Brooklyn Museum, New York. Partial gift of Suzi and Andrew Booke Cohen in memory of Ilene R. Booke and in honor of Arnold L. Lehman, Mary Smith Dorward Fund, and William K. Jacobs, Jr. Fund (2015.53). © 2005 Kehinde Wiley. Used by permission

Page 41: **Yinka Shonibare CBE**, *Butterfly Kid (Girl) IV*, 2017.
Fiberglass mannequin, Dutch wax printed cotton textile, silk, metal, globe, and steel baseplate, 125 × 79 × 95 cm (49¼ × 31⅛ × 37½ in.). © Yinka Shonibare CBE. All Rights Reserved, DACS/Artimage 2021. Image courtesy Goodman Gallery, Johannesburg. Photo Stephen White & Co.

Page 45: **Faith Ringgold**, *Tar Beach (Part I of Woman on a Bridge series)*, 1988.
Acrylic on canvas, bordered with printed, painted, quilted, and pieced cloth, 189.5 × 174 cm (74⅝ × 68½ in.). Solomon R. Guggenheim Museum, New York. Gift, Mr. and Mrs. Gus and Judith Lieber, 1988. © Faith Ringgold/ARS, NY and DACS, London, Courtesy ACA Galleries, New York, 2021

ABOUT THE AUTHOR

Sharna Jackson writes books and games for young people—mostly about art, artists, and mysteries. Her first novel, *High Rise Mystery* (2019), has won many awards, including the Waterstones Children's Book Prize for the Best Book for Younger Readers in 2020. Before this, Sharna worked in art galleries and museums, including Site Gallery in Sheffield, and Tate in London. She lives on an old ship in Rotterdam in the Netherlands.

ABOUT THE ILLUSTRATOR

Marilyn Esther Chi is a UK based illustrator who takes inspiration from anything and everything. The aim is to always create something that will be cherished and exudes wonderment.

ABOUT THE CONSULTANT

Dr. Zoé Whitley is the Director of Chisenhale Gallery in London. She co-curated the landmark exhibition *Soul of a Nation: Art in the Age of Black Power*, which toured venues in London and the U.S. between 2017 and 2020. She earned her PhD under the supervision of artist Professor Lubaina Himid. Zoé is the author of *The Graphic World of Paul Peter Piech*, and children's art activity book *Meet the Artist: Frank Bowling*.

Black Artists Shaping the World © 2021 and 2024 Thames & Hudson Ltd, London

This abridged, illustrated edition published in 2024

Text © 2021 and 2024 Sharna Jackson

Illustrations by Marilyn Esther Chi © 2024 Marilyn Esther Chi

Artwork reproductions see pp. 47

Consultancy by Dr. Zoé Whitley

First published in the United States of America in 2024 by Thames & Hudson Inc., 500 Fifth Avenue, New York, New York 10110

Library of Congress Control Number 2024932826

ISBN 978-0-500-65340-1

Printed and bound in China by C & C Offset Printing Co. Ltd

Be the first to know about our new releases, exclusive content and author events by visiting
thamesandhudson.com
thamesandhudsonusa.com
thamesandhudson.com.au

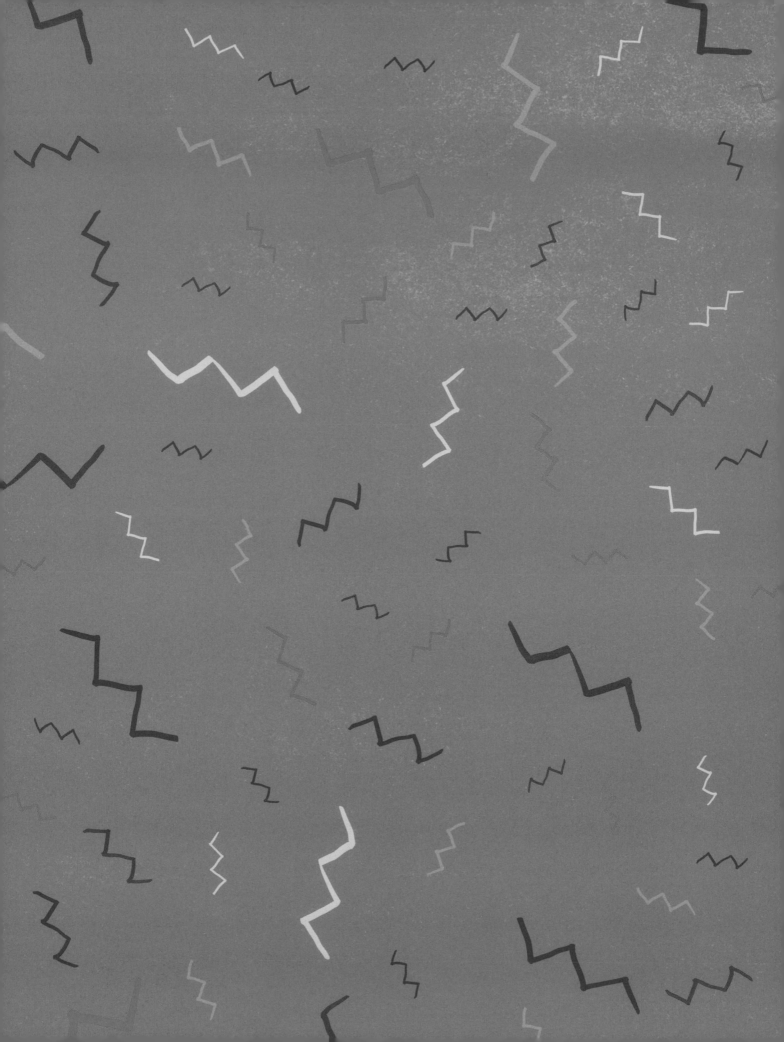